Marc Riboud

I for Imagine

Catherine

Chaine

Translated by Linda Asher

Tara Books

P for Prologue

What kind of alphabet book is this? The alphabet is a very particular organisation of meaning, a way of acquainting the reader—usually a child—with language, objects and associations. *I for Imagine* uses the conventions of the alphabet book, but for entirely unprecedented ends. The reader who is addressed here is not necessarily a child, although older children will enjoy going through this book, particularly with an adult. The words made by alphabets work here as pointers, nudging the viewer towards unexpected ways of reading photographs. They are more than captions, which place images in a context. They are escorts and narrators, free to move between suggesting particular meanings and playing with ineffable associations. They name not just objects, but ideas, reflections, emotions and concepts. Together with the captions, they form a rich web of relations around the image. *I for Imagine* is at once reflective and playful, lyrical and funny, a world of endless stories woven around moments of grace, sorrow and joy.

Sometimes words and images seem to combine in a relatively simple fashion. Consider, for example, *J for Joy*. An ecstatically happy girl leans out of a car. But then we read the caption and realise that the photograph was taken on the occasion of the Algerian independence from France in 1962. We notice the flag that the girl is holding. And the emotion begins to be placed within a particular political and temporal situation, turning into a moment that associates joy not only with everyday happiness, but also with struggle and freedom. The image and the word mirror each other, deepening the resonances of individual, national and historical memory.

R for Road seems quite literal as well. But this is no ordinary road: it is the Khyber Pass, which has determined so much of the Indian subcontinent's history. 'Road' is now in capital letters in our mind, and we pause to take in more of the picture, the wonderfully incongruous handmade sign, of animals and vehicles that have moved along this inhospitable path through past and present.

Other words are more obliquely chosen, one possibility among many—and yet the choice of a particular word turns out to be whimsically apt. *T for Turban* is one of our favourites, as is *B for Bottom*. *M for Mercy* adds a warm inflection to a strong—and justly famous—photograph. *C for Curious*: what could be a more delicious way of interpreting what all these different people are upto? We see, literally, that curiosity is a very universal human emotion, cutting through age and context. Here the visual and verbal meanings act on each other through an additional device: the juxaposition of particular images.

F for Factory and *F for Fatigue* work together as well, and effortlessly manage something formidable—they invoke an entire politics of labour. So by placing the individual photograph into a narrative sequence, image, word and meaning become part of an open ended collaboration, bringing us close to that rare thing: a deeply satisfying experience of the book form.

I for Imagine is a tribute to a way of seeing as well as an expression of it. The photographs featured in this book are from the vast oeuvre of renowned Magnum contributor Marc Riboud. Known for his capturing of what can be called 'the instinctive moment', his vision is strong yet compassionate, managing

to be poetic and gently humorous at the same time. Most of them are of parts of the world as it was in the 1950s and 1960s: Afghanistan, China, Cuba, Ghana, India, Turkey and Vietnam... each of these countries was caught in a spiral of change during this decade and Riboud's eye has kept pace with the changing times, carefully and with much empathy. His pictures of Indian life are both iconic as well as startling: a film director cranking a camera, labourers on a ladder hauling sand and stone, a camel market at the end of a long haggling day, boats on the Ganga in Benares... images which recall both Orientalist timelessness as well as the historic present. In either instance, wrenched from the habitual and the familiar, we experience both pleasure and knowledge. We learn to relish the intense human moment, even as we acknowledge the durable power of the iconic image.

This tussle between the familiar and the new, nostalgia and history, that these photos induce in the viewer is particularly strongest with images from times and places that have since changed dramatically. The eloquent shots of China in the 1950s and 1960s, capturing as they do the pathos, warmth and energy of the vast human drama of the revolution and its aftermath, appear doubly meaningful—their 'real time' emotions sit uneasily with our retrospective knowledge of that nation's history—and we are left with a sense of hopeless wonder. This is true of the pictures from Afghanistan as well—recalling in a way that they perhaps did not for the viewer of these pictures in the 1950s, a world that has not heeded or been allowed to heed its moments of poise and loveliness.

Formally, Riboud's images are perfectly composed, with an unerring sense of geometry. He recalls that when he was young, the great Henri Cartier Bresson told him that the best way to judge the lines of a good photograph was to look at it upside down. These images achieve that formal rigour in an almost inborn fashion, holding form and content in a natural, almost effortless balance.

Riboud's gaze is similar: his camera is leisurely, entranced with beauty but not seduced into ignoring the poignancy and unevenness of lives. He moves gently in time, and what he decides to capture is almost immediately sequenced into history. He focuses unerringly on the historic moment: whether it is images of Algerian independence or anti-Vietnam protests. At other times, the context is not obviously historical at first glance so much as with hindsight, as in his pictures of Ghana and India, with their particular ways of living and being. His version of the 'global'—as we would call it today—is through an evocation of the human condition in all it's variety, historically specific and yet transcending its context.

This way of seeing belongs to a time when the photographer was a bearer of memory, and the photograph appeared able to capture the burden of existential and historical truth (even if it did not always do so). In times like ours, when an exhausting array of images are beamed at us constantly, we are less hopeful or idealistic about representation or truth. Riboud's way of seeing pauses time, if only for a moment, slowing us down to a pace that allows us to stop, observe and relish the moment in all its richness and ambiguity before we deign to capture it.

V. Geetha and Gita Wolf
Tara Books

Introduction

"In theory," grownups write alphabet books to teach children their letters. I say "in theory" because grownups don't always tell the truth. Or anyhow, not the whole truth. In my case, for example, I'll tell you right off: I made this alphabet book for my own pleasure, and yours too—to share the pleasure with you. We should say, by the way, that it's very important and very hard to please yourself, and it would take an ABC book with every possible joy in it to make people a little less sad.

But to get back to our letters. How do these small black marks, lined up in a row like odd little sparrows on telephone wires, manage to make us so happy? Well, simply because they have always joined together to form thousands of words, and with those words we can name everything: what we see, what we hear, what we smell, what we feel, what we love, what we hate, and all the rest. Most of the time, of course, we speak these words rather than write them. If you come across a lion in the street, for instance on the way to school, you're going to shout his name to chase him away, or murmur it to beg him not to eat you, but since it's an emergency you're not going to write to him.

And yet, knowing how to write words with a good sharp pencil or a nice pen can give you enormous pleasure. Different and even greater pleasure than the joy of talking. I can't list all the joys of writing because there are too many, and each of you will experience them in your own way, but as soon as you begin to write, you will probably feel how nice it is to grip a pen in your three fingers and set it to tracing the shapes of letters—very definite shapes. They recur over and over in the world but, drawn by your own hand, they can be recognized among all the letters drawn by your friends because, as soon as you start

writing, you will have "your" handwriting, unlike any other. And you will discover very soon that the words a person writes often come out stronger, more exact, more precious, than the words he speaks, and that there are also words we don't dare say but we can write, words of love in particular. And sometimes, words of anger.

I don't know why I began by talking about the joys of writing rather than about the joys of reading. Perhaps because those second sort take longer to develop, and because letters might not at first look to you like nice sparrows but more like dark, stern, disagreeable eyebrows, frowning in all directions, and impossible to understand. The business of learning to read is often like the huge wave that those kids in Ghana (*W for Wave*) have to get through before they can start catching wonderful fish in a sea all calm and warm, with exactly the right amount of salt.

It was to help you get past that big wave as well that I have put together this alphabet book with Marc Riboud, my favorite photographer, who is also—no secrets—my husband. With him you'll kill two birds with one stone: exploring letters and words, you will also learn to read the world. As you turn the pages of this ABC, you will follow him over the paths he has traveled on foot or on wheels; along with him you will gaze at things he has touched, and loved, enough to pick them out, set them apart, save them, transform them into photographs. The words will turn into images, you will "see" the sadness in the eyes of a young Chinese soldier, the Indian boats in the twilight, the grace of an African girl standing in her cabin doorway. You will discover beauty in places we don't perceive it because that's not where we expected it—in the tangled weeds of a garden,

in a plastic bag that becomes a weird rabbit, in three little girls huddled together against the dust and the harsh wind.

Little by little you will "hear" the pictures, because they speak a silent language like the words in books. From one photograph to the next you will come to understand how Marc Riboud looks at the life around him and at people with humor, with tenderness, and with that astonishment you feel yourself because, as photographed by him, everything seems new, seen for the first time.

And just as he chose to photograph a mischievous little Chinese boy, a teenager dreaming in an Afghani teahouse, or the beautiful gesture of the child launching his kite into the skies above Istanbul; just as I chose the pictures for this ABC book from among thousands of his others, you too will choose "your" photos, and you will remake the world in your own way and to your own taste.

Thanks to these pictures, these letters, these words, you will be that boy washing down elephants in the waters of the Ganges River, or the one parading like a young sultan on the back of the great animal in Jaipur. The sad gaze of the very dignified English woman or the angry look of the turbaned man in Bangkok may remind you of someone you love. To look at a photo is always to recall or invent a story. What's become of the Nepalese boy leaping so happily into the Mekong River, or the little scamp photographing the photographer with just his fingers? What are their lives like? Each one of you will make up whatever you wish in your head or—who knows?—maybe write it, with the letters you learn as you turn these pages, back and forth, dreaming...

Catherine Chaine

A for Acrobat

Paris, France, 1953

Istanbul, Turkey, 1955

for Asleep

Paris, France, 1990

for Abdomen

Old Delhi, India, 1956

for Alone

Strike in Liverpool. England, 1954

Beijing, China, 1957

B for Books

Riyadh, Saudi Arabia, 1974

for Bowler Hat

London, England, 1954

for Bottom

Forbidden City. Beijing, China, 1957

for Boat

Accra, Ghana, 1960

C for Cameraman

Calcutta, India, 1956

for Couple

Conakry, Guinea, 1960

for Cheerful

Paris, France, 1974

for Curious

Istanbul, Turkey, 1955

London, England, 1954

D for Dinosaur

London, England, 1954

for Donkey

Khyber Pass, Afghanistan, 1955

Lhasa, Tibet, 1985

for Dream

Kabul, Afghanistan, 1955

On the train from Guangzhou to Beijing. China, 1957

E for Elephants

Benares, India, 1956

Benares, India, 1956

for Eat

Anshan, China, 1957

for Eyes

Shanghai, China, 2002

for Evening

Desert in South Algeria, Algeria, 1960

F for Flight

Beijing, China, 1957

for Factory

Anshan, China, 1957

for Fatigue

Havana, Cuba, 1963

Desert in North Kenya, Kenya, 1963

G for Giraffe

for Game

Istanbul, Turkey, 1955

Swayambhunath stupa, Kathmandu valley. Nepal, 1956

for Grace

Unknown village by the river Niger, Niger, 1963

Dubrovnik, Yugoslavia, 1954

for Group

Unknown village, North Vietnam, 1969

H for Hands

Tokyo, Japan, 1958

for Hammock

Conakry, Guinea, 1960

Hanoi, North Vietnam, 1969

for Herbs

Touraine, France, 2000

I for Imitate

Shanghai, China, 1995

for Intense

Beijing, China, 1957

for Ice

Moscow, Russia, 1960

Bangkok, Thailand, 1969

J for Jump

Villeurbanne, France, 1984

Conakry, Guinea, 1960

Shanghai, China, 2002

for Joy

Algiers, Algeria. July 1962, Independence Day.

K for Kayak

Accra, Ghana, 1960

for Keel

Saint-Nazaire, France, 1959

for Kimono

Tokyo, Japan, 1958

for Kiss

London, England, 1954

Southend, England, 1955

L for Lovers

for Lazy

Kathmandu, Nepal, 1956

for Ladder

Chandigarh, India, 1956

M for Mother

Tanganyka, 1961

for Market

Camels market in Nagor. India, 1956

for Miner

Taiyuan, China, 1995

for Mess

Beijing, China, 1992

for Mercy

Protest against the war in Vietnam. Washington, USA, 1967

Unknown village in the North, Ghana, 1960

N for Naked

Prado Museum. Madrid, Spain, 1988

Prado Museum. Madrid, Spain, 1988

for Nap

Accapulco, Mexico, 1969

O for Oar

North-east coast, India, 1956

for Oilfield

Baku, Azerbaijan, 1998

for Old

Hong Kong, China, 1956

for Oxygen

Moscow, Russia, 1961

P for Push

Accra, Ghana, 1960

Shanghai, China, 1957

for Pond

Pontlevoy, Touraine, France, 1963

for Peacock

Jaipur, India, 1956

Q for Quarrel

Accra, Ghana, 1960

for Quicken

Shanghai, China, 1965

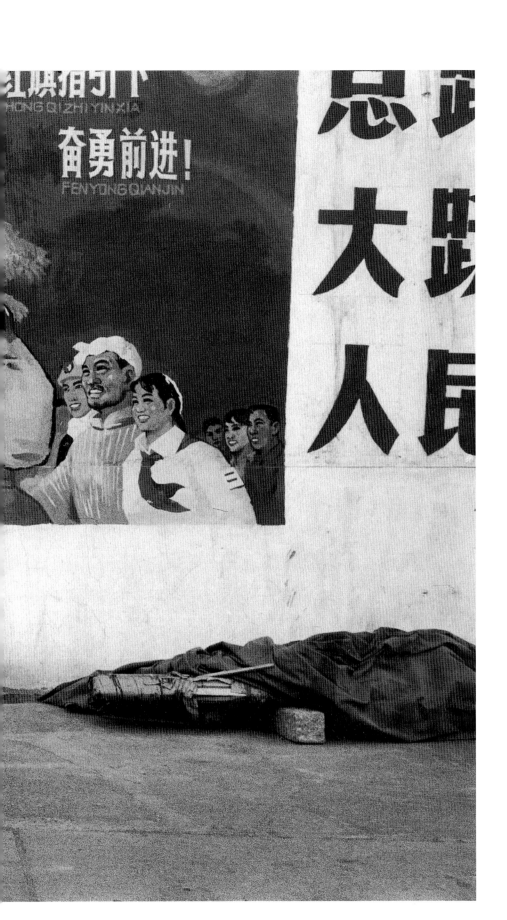

for Quay

Shanghai, China, 2002

for Quilt

Khyber Pass, Afghanistan, 1955

Cappadocia, Turkey, 1955

R for Rock

for Rabbit

Shanghai, China, 2002

for Road

Khyber Pass, Afghanistan, 1955

for Rowing

Accra, Ghana, 1960

Java, Indonesia, 1956

S for Sail

for Shadow

Touraine, France, 2008

for Sad

People's Palace. Beijing, China, 1971

for Son

In the steppes. Mongolia, 1965

On a boat on a little river. North Vietnam, 1969

for Snow

Anchorage, USA, 1959

Forbidden City. Beijing, China, 1957

T for Twilight

Benares, India, 1956

Vietnam, 1969

for Turban

Calcutta, India, 1956

for Turtle

On the road from Ankara to Kayseri. Turkey, 1955

for Tenderness

Unknown village, North Vietnam, 1969

Catherine Chaine and her mother.
Hennequeville, Normandy, 1950

On the road from Tabriz to Teheran. Iran, 1955

U for Unjust

Accra, Ghana, 1960

for Uprising

May '68. Paris, France, 1968

May '68. Paris, France, 1968

for Upperclass

British Museum. London, England, 1954

London, England, 1954

V for Veil

Algiers, Algeria, 1969

for Viewfinder

Kathmandu, Nepal, 1956

for Victory

Algiers, Algeria. July 1962, Independence Day.

Accra, Ghana, 1960

W for Wave

for Windows

Beijing, China, 1965

for Weight

Beijing, China, 1957

X for X

Southend, England, 1954

Shanghai, China, 2002

Accra, Ghana, 1960

Y for Young

for Yell

Anti-american demonstration. Beijing, China, 1965

Johannesburg, South Africa, 1998

Z for Zap

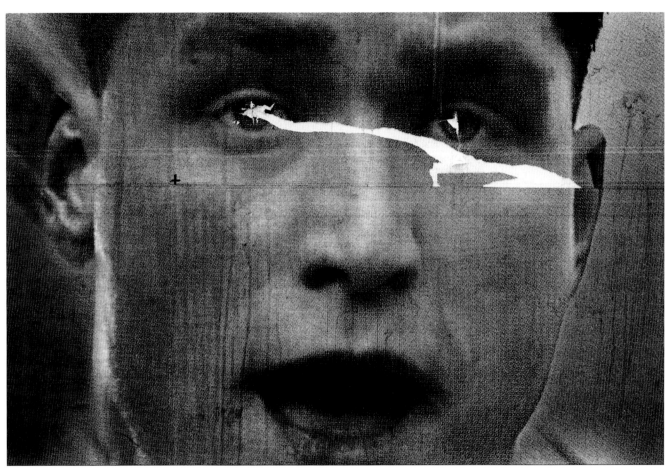

Bratislava, Slovakia, 1994

for Zen

Angkor, Cambodia, 1969

I for Imagine
Copyright © Tara Books Pvt. Ltd. 2010
For the photographs: Marc Riboud
For the introduction: Catherine Chaine
For this edition: Tara Books Pvt. Ltd., India *www.tarabooks.com*
& Tara Publishing Ltd., UK *www.tarabooks.com/uk*

Design: Martin Argyroglo Callias Bey
Production: C. Arumugam
Printed through Asia Pacific Offset, China
Published in association with the French Embassy in India

Photo credits: wherever possible, we have identified the city
and country where a photograph was taken. We have followed
the convention of retaining the names of countries as they existed
at the time the pictures were taken.

With thanks to Small World, our group of publishers, for making this
interaction possible. Les Trois Ourses, France; Petra Ediciones, Mexico;
One Stroke, Japan; Tara Books, India.

ISBN 978-93-80340-10-4

Publisher's Note
French Focus is a new series of visual arts titles published by Tara
Books in association with the French Embassy in India.

Some of the most daring and creative visual books being published
today come from France, and over the years, Tara's books have
found homes with some of the finest French publishers.

We hope to reciprocate with this series, and introduce readers
to our favourites—from art books for adults to picture books for
children, or indeed books that straddle genres and can only be
described as 'Beaux Livres' or 'Beautiful Books'.